THE
FUTURE
of the
SELF

THE
FUTURE
of the
SELF

Joanna Nadin

MELVILLE HOUSE UK
LONDON

THE FUTURE of the SELF

First published in 2024 by
Melville House UK
Suite 2000
16/18 Woodford Road
London E7 0HA

and

Melville House Publishing
46 John Street
Brooklyn, NY 11201

mhpbooks.com @melvillehouse

A CIP catalogue record for this book is available from the British Library

UK: 978-1-911545-69-9
US: 978-1-68589-133-6

1 3 5 7 9 10 8 6 4 2

Printed in Denmark by Nørhaven, Viborg
Typesetting by Roland Codd

PART 1
The Backstory of Self

A caveat

Before we begin, a disclaimer.

I'm not a psychologist or neuroscientist, nor even a philosopher. Yes, I have a PhD in the nature of self, but in relation to young adult (YA) literature; I'm not the kind of doctor who is useful on an aeroplane. I'm a novelist and sometime speechwriter. I mostly let others do the hard work of research, then, like a gold digger, I pan their insightful, if sometimes dry, findings for the shiny stuff that I can turn into a story or a soundbite. And that is, effectively, what I'm doing here. I'm pressing the work of greater minds than mine into service to tell the story of self – where it is now, and where it might be heading. And, most importantly, why that matters.

This story, though, is unlike any others I've conjured. It straddles several genres, from sixties psychedelia to coming-of-age tale to dystopian sci-fi. There's no clear inciting incident, but a plethora of changes that have all played a part. It also opens with a single, mostly likeable protagonist – our hero, the 'true self'. But, while I won't spoil the story by telling you if they survive or not, I will admit that we end in a potentially infinite crowd scene. There is, though, redemption of sorts, and I may have thrown in a couple of dragons along the way for effect.

So, sit back and enjoy the ride, as I take you on a quest not just to slay those dragons, but to find your own future self.

A 'self' obsession

It is summer 1978, the evening air still redolent with overheated tarmac, the mint-green Tupperware beaker of water next to my bed tainted by a residue of orange squash and plastic. Downstairs the grown-ups are discussing someone called Margaret Thatcher, who looks and sounds worryingly like my Aunty Peggy (a woman I would not want in charge of anything, given her ban on children in the drawing room and inclusion of fishpaste sandwiches at high tea). But up here, rigid under a garish duvet cover, the eight-year-old me has more important matters to mind. She has just, in what will be her first epiphanic moment, realised the sheer incredibility of her existence as a tangible, singular being. There can't be that many people in the world, she thinks. A thousand, maybe; two thousand at most. So, the very fact she is on earth at all seems almost impossible to comprehend and renders her definitely 'special'. But what is troubling her is not how she *came to be*, but what she will *come to be*. For, if there are so few people alive at all, the self she is had better be a good one. But what *is* her 'self'?

She knows what her mother thinks it is.

'There are pretty girls, and there are *clever* girls, Joanna. You are a *clever* girl.'

Being clever is important, she thinks. But she would like to be pretty too. And more. She would like to be funny, sassy, ingenious. More specifically, she would like to be George in the *Famous Five*, or the eponymous Heidi, or, whisper it, Cinderella – a name that tends to elicit sighs from her mother (something to do with excessive dresses and possibly false expectations of men). In any case, she had better get on with choosing her 'self' quick; she needs to pick one and stick to it, because it is only *one* we get after all, isn't it?

And so begins what will turn out to be a long and arduous journey to find a better self. First, I don the mantles of the various inhabitants of Malory Towers – practical Darrell with her flashes of anger, which feel all too familiar; class joker Alicia; quiet but courageous Mary-Lou. (Though never Gwendoline Mary – I'm clever, not pretty, remember?) Then, when I have outgrown the pages of Blyton, I progress to Dickens and du Maurier (Who *doesn't* want to run off with smugglers? I reason) before, somewhere around the age of fifteen, emerging, blinking, from the dim-lit aisles of the library to

pick models from the ranks hanging around outside
the sixth form common room – a New Romantic, a
Goth, a psychobilly carrying a King Kurt single like
a talisman, its Woolworth's sticker intact.

Next, what feels like a decade behind everyone
else, we acquire a VHS player (our nearest cinema is
an unbreachable thirteen miles away) and I begin to
imagine myself on the silver screen: Andie in *Pretty
in Pink* – the girl literally from the wrong side of
the tracks who wins the heart of the rich kid with
her outlandish dress sense and love of vinyl. Baby in
Dirty Dancing who gets to save the world, as well as
dance the cha-cha-cha with Patrick Swayze. Literally
anyone from *Mystic Pizza* – Jojo who shares my
name (a sign, right?), my temper, and my suspicions
that marriage is a swizz; Daisy who (again) wins
the heart of the rich kid but also bests him at pool;
bookish babysitter Kat who falls for the father of
her charge (I know, I know – unthinkable now, but
in my defence it was the 1980s and I was a teenager,
and a fool).

Later, I change career with determination and
frequency: actress, circus trainee, radio newsreader,
political adviser. These are guises I try out for size,
all the while terrified that what I fear is my 'true' self
– the smart but plain one my mother has painted me

as – will out. But still this does not stop me, because, helpless, I march to the mantra in my head that beats out the question 'Who am I?'

Inevitable, then, or it seems so to me, that I will turn this obsession, and quick-change ability, into a career.

ı) ▸ ▸ ▶ ▶

I admitted at the beginning that I'm a novelist. More specifically, for many years I was known as a writer of young adult fiction, my stock-in-trade sending countless adolescents on quests to find their 'one true self'. To work out not *what* they want to do, but *who* they will be when they leap, like Holden Caulfield, from the fields of rye of childhood over that cliff into the unknown but presumably dull or dystopian landscape of 'being a grown up'. I dealt, frequently and unashamedly, in cheap metamorphosis scenes. You know the ones: Olivia Newton-John goes from *Grease*'s goody-two-shoes, swing-skirted Sandra Dee to leather-clad Sandy, stubbing out a cigarette with the toe of her red stiletto (Tell me about it, Stud). Ally Sheedy gets the Molly Ringwald treatment at *The Breakfast Club*, taking her from allegedly repellent dandruff-ridden emo to Emilio Estevez's personal cheerleader. Art geek Laney Boggs takes off her glasses and suddenly *She's All That* and Freddie

Prinze Junior is hanging around for more than a bet, hair improbably gelled and tongue lolling.

God, how the teenage me had longed for this to happen. To go from brittle, beige chrysalis to Technicolor butterfly. And, God, how I'd tried. I'd started young, of course, with the contents of a well-stocked dressing-up box. Clothed in leftover hessian from one of my mother's many craft projects, I would quickly don a cardboard crown when my fairy god-mother – a conscripted but willing little brother – transformed me into the princess I longed to be. When hormones set in and I acquired a second-hand stereo, my gaze turned to musical chameleons Bolan and Bowie. I wanted them and I wanted to be them – to have that confidence to cast off sub-urban or working-class childhood through clothes, make-up and a change of name. At seventeen I fell for Frank N. Furter and *The Rocky Horror Show*'s exhortation 'don't dream it, be it', escaping small-town Essex for Friday nights at the Prince Charles cinema off Leicester Square, along with hundreds of other wannabes and wish-they-weres dressed up for the singalong version of the film.

Makeover television offered up more fodder. As an eleven-year-old I had longed to sit on the hot pleather banquette in the window of Hair By Us and watch the Essex girls being permed, bobbed and blow-dried. I daren't ask my mother to be allowed this treat for fear of sounding 'weird' or 'lesbian' (the worst insults I could imagine at that point; now, of course, badges of honour). But in my twenties I found myself free to take in such transformations at leisure, and in private. Shows like *Ten Years Younger*, *What Not to Wear* and *The Swan* depicted ugly ducklings like me being transformed, all building up to that 'mirror moment' when their new look would be revealed and they (and we) would gasp in delight.

The problem was I had a horrible sense that, like the clock striking midnight casting Cinderella back in rags, or the curtain being drawn back in Oz to reveal a withered facsimile of a wizard, someone would switch on a light and my 'true self' – the merely clever girl – would be revealed.

Hadn't it already?

ı ̨ ̨ ̨ ▶ ▶

Jump back again to 1984 and my first village disco. It is an auspicious occasion, heralded by furtive whispers in class and a slew of phone calls in which my friend Ruth and I ascertain which boys will be there, and which might deign to snog us on the dance floor (or do more in the toilets or outside in the phone box). But if I am going to be kissed (or more) I need to look the part, and that means make-up, and something more daring to wear than jeans and a hand-me-down Burton's shirt from Peter Marsh over the road (the shame!). And so I fashion myself a transformation. Wearing a kilt rolled up into a miniskirt, a school shirt with the collar cut off and new pink buttons sewn on, a slick of all-the-rage hypothermic Boots 17 'Twilight Teaser' on my lips, I tread down the rough-carpeted stairs of our 1970s estate home with all the fear and anticipation of my longed-to-be Cinderella awaiting judgment from the wicked stepmother. My own actual mother, while not exactly wicked, is a harsh critic.

'What on earth do you think you look like?'

I stutter out an 'I don't know' to be met with what, to me, amounts to eternal damnation.

'You look absurd. You're not that sort of girl. You don't look like you.'

And the scene ends, as it invariably did, with my 'wiping that stuff off and putting something more sensible on'.

I didn't want to believe it. But if my mother had said it, then surely it had to be true? These clothes weren't 'me'. Make-up was just a pathetic attempt to cover glaring 'truth': nothing more than Lewis

Carroll's Duchess putting clothes on a pig and pretending it was a baby. The lesson was clear: I should learn to accept who I am.

And so, despite the brief thrill of the makeover, that is what my YA books taught: a form of self-acceptance. Like so many writers before me and after, I exhorted my heroines to 'just be yourself' and to revel in the original 'true' version. Which, I wondered, was worse though: promising a potentially doomed fairytale transformation or forcing someone to 'stay in their lane'?

〉 〉 〉 〉 〉 〉

Cut to 2014, and I'm in the early stages of drafting the novel that will form part of my doctoral thesis – a sort of *Mean Girls* meets *Heathers* meets *The Riot Club*. And, as I prepare to tell yet another heroine to 'accept herself' I begin to ask questions:

Why should they, or I for that matter, accept ourselves if we don't like the selves we're currently inhabiting? After all, these may be ones we've inherited, in terms of class or genetics, and might not feel like 'me' at all.

Why have my own changes of appearance, as well as career – a veritable Cher Horowitz revolving wardrobe in *Clueless* – been dismissed by friends and acquaintances as something unsavoury or

untrustworthy, as 'insincere' in the mould of Dorian
Gray, or, once by a fellow politico, as 'Mitty-like'?

Why, ultimately, do any of us have to have a 'true
self' at all?

I got the answers, at least at first, from another
novelist.

▶ ▶ ▶ ▶ ▶ ▶

A friend of a more-than-friend, I am introduced to
novelist Emily Mackie in a Bristol café and manage
to stammer out an elevator pitch.

'It's about the quest for identity,' I say. 'You know,
the usual. "Be yourself", "find yourself". The whole
Disney, high-school-movie thing. Only . . .' Was I
going to admit it? I was. 'I'm going in circles. Like
the whole thing's a trick, a wild goose chase.'

Mackie nods and I feel the thrill of validation like
a blood rush. 'It's bogus,' she says. 'There is no "self".'

And there I see it: the first flash of my magic
amulet.

It wasn't mere coincidence; I had hankered after a
meeting with Mackie for a while, on the back of my
fascination with her first novel *And This Is True*. But
that rainy, cold afternoon on the Gloucester Road,
amongst the dregs of coffee, crumbs of churros and
smears of chocolate sauce, felt like nothing less than

serendipity, my very own inciting incident. Because Mackie, it transpired, was as obsessed with self as I, but at this point far better read.

In the midst of researching her second novel, *In Search of Solace* – an investigation into the very nature of identity – Mackie had questioned whether or not self existed as an essential, singular thing, and come up with a resounding 'no'. Her novel would posit self as: (a) mutable – meaning malleable, or able to change at will; (b) multiple – meaning there isn't just one 'self' but many, and (c) a construct of those around us, who shape those selves just as much as we do.

'Huh?' I might think, if only in my head.

'Yeah, basically I don't exist except through you.'

I must look embarrassingly baffled, because she frowns and gestures for my pen. 'You need to read *The Self Illusion*,' she says, jotting the name down for me on the back of a napkin. 'Bruce Hood. It'll change the way you see everything. That and Baggini's *The Ego Trick*. I'd start with them, if I were you.'

So I did, and for that I owe Mackie a debt, as these two books became my lodestars throughout the journey of researching and writing my PhD, one YA and three 'adult' novels, as well as this work of 'fact'. More than that, it altered my sense of self profoundly and irrevocably. Because what they posit, as Mackie summed up for me, is that self, as we think of it, simply does not exist.

'I' do not exist

Look in the mirror, or even just close your eyes, and who do you see?

'Me', right? A single, unique being – the same single, unique being who's captured in a handstand aged seven in the family album; pinioned to the fridge in an embarrassing adolescent snapshot; framed in silver on the mantelpiece, possibly drunk or hungover, but happy in wedding dress or tails. The same single, unique being who woke up yesterday, and will wake up, hopefully, tomorrow, to eat the same breakfast and brush the same teeth with the same slightly splayed toothbrush and forget, again, to get a new one. Yes, the hairstyle has changed and even the opinions, but it's still undeniably 'me', isn't it?

Only where, in that body of mine, is the 'me' located?

As a child I assumed that 'self' nestled like a pearl somewhere in the soft oyster of my innards; that it resembled, perhaps, a sliver of overused soap – thin, grey, translucent – and was located either in my brain or behind my heart. I didn't question its existence; it just 'was', in the same way that God and the tooth fairy just 'were'. Sure, I'd never seen any of them, but they must be around somewhere, had to be, or else what on earth was the point?

A few years later, as I grimly and dramatically dissected first a toad, then a rat, for my A level biology and labelled the contents, this essential part – the very 'toadness' or 'ratness' of them – seemed to be missing. What if, I worried, like the tooth fairy and God (who had recently been proven to me to be no more than carrot and stick in the grown-up tool-kit), the solid self, that particular sliver of me-ness, didn't actually exist in my body at all?

You know the answer to this already, of course: it doesn't.

Our bodies aren't even stable or, more worryingly, entirely ours. While our DNA is indeed unique (even, I was disappointed to learn, in identical twins), our cells are constantly changing, being renewed. The average cell lasts less than a decade; some are replaced daily. We are, effectively, a walking, talking Ship of Theseus, that paradox whereby parts of a ship are slowly replaced over time until no original parts remain, and yet its identity seemingly stays the same. Or Trigger's infamous broom from the TV series *Only Fools and Horses*, whose wooden entirety – handle and bristles – though it looks the same and is still serving the same purpose to no apparent detriment, has been replaced several times over. Or, perhaps, a band – Fleetwood Mac or Fairport Convention – whose line-ups are manifold and pliable though they assume the same name and are seemingly accorded the same reverence (I concede the same might not be said of, for example, Bucks Fizz, though I will not hear a word said against Sugababes). Add to that the fact that the majority of cells in our bodies aren't even human. We are host to thousands of species of bacteria and viruses, some of which have the ability to control our thoughts and actions.

'But it's still "me"!' you may cry. 'I look the same and think the same!'

Well, parasitic DNA aside, fair point. And besides, what does it matter? Well, not much, except in the search for the elusive 'self'.

'Well, check my brain, then,' you say. 'It has to be in there!'

The thing is I did. Or rather, cleverer men and women, with the required qualifications and tools to do it, did. And they're all in agreement: it's not in there either. Because the pearl of self, as you and I think of it – a solid, stable, singular entity; something locatable and quantifiable – simply does not exist. What we think of as 'self' – that essential 'me-ness' – is an illusion, a trick played by the mind to give us a sense of wholeness. Self is not an object, but a construct or process; it is a *story* that we tell ourselves about ourselves.

The story of self

The argument goes like this: each of us has to a greater or lesser extent that feeling of 'me-ness': of both existence as a separate being, and of the specific nature of that being – our 'character'. And that me-ness is remarkably enduring, despite our ever-changing circumstances, tastes and relationships. But here's the thing: that me-ness is not something the brain *possesses*, it is something the brain *does*; a 'symphony', as Bruce Hood describes it, played by the orchestra of processes in the brain.

Julian Baggini calls this the 'ego trick'; for Hood it is the 'self illusion', but both put forward the same idea that wholeness is effect rather than cause, as the mind quietly manages to convince us that we are unified. And it manages to do that because we are all masters of fiction, flicking through the snapshot album of memories and weaving them into a convincing narrative that helps us pretend we are one coherent person. It is this narrative that creates the feeling of unity, a feeling so compelling that we can't help but perceive ourselves as solid objects, unchangeable as a brick or a bicycle, when in fact we are fluid and, crucially, malleable. Because this narrative isn't an unchangeable text, but can be revised and rewritten, moulded like Play-Doh or Plasticine to absorb inconsistences and maintain coherence.

'Crikey,' you might say (I did). But wait, there's more!

We don't even write this fiction all by ourselves. Self is not a monologue, constructed by our mind in isolation, but the product of an ongoing conversation; it is *dialogic*, born of our interactions with significant (and less significant) others.

The idea that we are partly what others perceive might strike you as the stuff of adolescent nightmare: a damning confirmation that looks matter, that labels stick, that we are what we wear, say, listen to. The evidence is, however, overwhelming. Hood and Baggini, and a myriad of others, cast those with whom we interact – our family, friends, idols, even fictional characters – in the role of meaning-givers. But, before you hit the self-destruct button, it's important to point out that this doesn't render us puppets. Rather, it simply reveals that we're not driven exclusively from the inside out, as we vainly like to think of ourselves. Instead, the self we project onto the world is also a product of that world. So the people with whom we interact are, effectively, our 'co-creators'. They help make us who we are. In other words, we think of our self, at least in part, according to what they think, or, more precisely, according to what we think they think. In simple terms, other people – and by extension, their opinions – matter. But, and this is key, this isn't some sort of weakness, the sign of a withered or atrophied self, easily manipulated, able to do no more than follow the herd. First, because no one is doing any deliberate manipulation in this scenario; it occurs largely on the level of the subconscious. Secondly, because the fact that we subconsciously take on board elements of other people is actually favourable. A strength. Necessary, even.

Let's look for a moment at 'mirror neurons'.

Mirror neurons are a type of brain cell that fire up not just when we do a certain action, for example when we eat an ice cream, but when we see someone else do the same action. The relatively recent discovery of these synapses was, at the time, likened in scientific significance to that of DNA. That might be overegging it slightly, but mirror neurons are undeniably important in our thinking about self.

To understand how they work, let's go back to a
lab in the mid-1990s and a bunch of monkeys with
(apologies) electrodes implanted into their brains.
When the monkeys handled food, a certain area
of the brain lit up – the premotor cortex. But it's
what happened next that's the game-changer: when
the monkeys saw the researchers handling food, the
same area of the brain lit up.

It works the same way in humans. These path-
ways effectively 'fire' when watching other people,
eliciting a mirroring action – a slip of our accent
perhaps, or our experiencing an identical emotion
as they recount a story. When we watch someone,
for example, kick a football, the part of our brain
that would fire if we actually kicked a football
fires anyway. We don't even need to see it; it works
when just thinking about it as well – reading fiction
is a great example of this, and a reason we should
do more of it, as what it encourages is, of course,
empathy. (I'll come back to this later, but a side note
here: this is partly why you'll often hear stories used
in speeches. They elicit empathy, they literally 'move'
people – in some cases to the polling booth – which
is, of course, the aim of any good rhetoric.)

For Hood this process is akin to resonance; he
compares it to the hard striking of a 'G' string in

a guitar showroom so that all the other 'G' strings begin to vibrate (an act I have yet to test the veracity of, but the analogy works so I'm having it). And this unconscious or subconscious mimicry, this attempt to 'fit in', is not a fault, nor merely pleasing, but rather a survival method designed to bring us together, to help us get along. Self is socially constructed in order for society to thrive. Whether it's unconscious mirroring, or the conscious drive to be one of the crowd (or, indeed, stand out from it), self is a two-way street.

Feeling better about losing your 'self' if it's in the common good? Well, I hope so. But brace yourself, because that's not all.

So far I've established that 'true self' – a hard, immutable pearl of 'me-ness' – just doesn't exist. It's a trick of the mind designed to help us feel stable (a useful, if not essential survival mechanism) when we are anything but. Because self is a story, and stories are, as we know, easily rewritten, and sometimes not by ourselves but in a subconscious dialogue with others around us. But – and this is where you will need to breathe deep – even the word 'dialogic' is misleading, because it's not one conversation, or negotiation, we have with the world but many (and in ever-increasing number, but I'm saving that joy for later). This leads me to what Baggini describes as the 'obvious' question, but which was, for me (a non-philosopher), revelatory: 'Once the idea of the unitary self is fractured, should we not take this one stage further and accept that, in the absence of a strongly singular "I", there must be a weakly multiple "we"?'

In other words, we all contain multiple selves.

I contain multitudes

'I come to feel more and more,' wrote Virginia Woolf to G.L. Dickinson, 'how difficult it is to collect myself into one Virginia.'

Same, Virginia, same. I am Joanna the children's writer. The adult novelist. The academic. The friend (many times over). The sometimes girlfriend (less happily, also manifold). The mother (thankfully only once). The ex-wife (likewise). I am Joanna the daughter. The sister. The neighbour. The union member. The mentor. The ex-politico. I am also, at various times (sometimes simultaneously), 'Jo', 'Joey', 'Jonads', 'Nadgers', 'Mushma', 'Aunty Monkey' and, rarely, Dr Nadin. And even within each named version there are myriad other 'subselves'. I am not the same Jo, for example, when I talk to old school-friends (from Conservative Essex) as I am when I talk to more recent ones (from left-leaning Bristol). I was not the same Jo with one partner, who worked in film and geeked out on the Muppets, as with the one that followed, who worked in politics and watched mostly the Parliament channel and *Breaking Bad*. That's not to say I switch identity completely, or 'lose myself'. More that certain sides of me come to the fore while others might be subconsciously (or otherwise) dampened.

But this idea of the self as manifold is one that, historically, has tended to be confined to psychiatric units, and in literary terms to gothic horror. From the doubling of Jekyll and Hyde, and Dorian Gray, on the page, to the split personalities of Sybil on the big screen, the popular view of multiple personality is as a psychopathological state, a disorder now known as 'Dissociative Identity' (DID). But, as Woolf suggested as early as the late 1920s, perhaps the idea of many selves isn't a strange aberration, but the natural state of human being.

⟩ ⟩ ⟩ ⟩ ⟩ ⟩

'I look how you want to look,' alter ego Stella tells 'host' Jude in my 2009 YA novel *Wonderland*. 'I talk how you want to talk. All the ways you wish you could be, that's me.' She's quoting of course, from

Fight Club. The film (and Chuck Palahniuk's original novel) is widely accepted as a portrayal of DID: Brad Pitt's Tyler Durden an alpha-male alter ego to Edward Norton's anonymous and very much beta narrator – a set-up I mirrored with gawky, awkward Jude and wild socialite Stella. But psychologist Steven Gold argues a different slant: he believes the film illustrates how modern life, which requires us to 'be' so many different things in so many different places, encourages a form of dissociation, or 'splitting'. He's not alone in seeing this multiplicity as 'normative'.

Selves, according to Rita Carter, a medical writer specialising in neuroscience, do not pre-exist but are conjured up by each of us in as great a number, as many different forms, and as frequently as needed. Just as Julian Baggini and Bruce Hood set out, these selves are created via dialogic interactions, each one producing a new self, which accumulate into what she terms a 'family'. Some of us have relatively small 'families' and some are more on the level of Disney's *Encanto* – like so many things, self is on a spectrum rather than being binary. And at least one of these selves will be a whole, rounded, fairly constant presence – what she terms 'majors' – while others are less well-defined and infrequent visitors (minors). Some (micros) may be no more than a 'vocal tic' or 'intrusive thought'. But we all, to a greater or lesser extent, have a myriad of these selves. And these identities are not 'fake' – a deliberately insincere act put on purely to manipulate – they are subconscious creations and are, in that sense, 'honest'. They are also, in this sense only, akin to the multiple 'alters' that can be delineated in DID.

In this brutal condition, an alter or number of alters is created in order to cope with – or block out – childhood trauma, often sexual abuse (in *Wonderland*, this was the death of Jude's mother). But in DID these alters do not usually share memory; they exist in separate, locked 'houses', whereas multiplicity of self is more what Carter terms an 'open-plan' arrangement. Carter isn't an outlier in this thinking either. There are numerous other researchers who use more or less effective analogies to describe a state of multiplicity – 'subselves', 'subpersonalities', a 'string of pearls', 'ego states'. What these concepts share is the idea that the right self is assumed for the right situation and those situations are on the increase as we interact with more and more people in more and more different ways. As such, far from being detrimental to our mental health, multiplicity is a natural adaptation to the connected world we now live in.

That doesn't mean it's easy. There are so many iterations of 'me' that the idea of a large party at which I might be required to play several or even all of these parts is daunting to the point that, instead of having a wedding, I eloped. Even book launches can render me mute as I find the switching of guises tiring, albeit not impossible. But it's something I have had to adapt to. And I'm going to have to get better at it in the future. We all are.

Where next?

So the self has gone the same way as the Easter Bunny, the tooth fairy, Father Christmas and, for me at least, God, Jesus and any other vague deity. That 'pearl' as we tend to think of it – singular, impermeable – does not exist. Instead, it is a story (or rather stories), told and retold as we shape ourselves to a fast-changing world.

As a writer, and apparent chameleon, I was buoyed by the discovery. I no longer had to pathologise someone who had two sides (or more) to them. Nor did I have to force happily transforming characters to 'revert to type'. However, I accept that it's not necessarily an easy pill to swallow (my publishers certainly didn't agree with me). The problem is, singular unified selves are appealing. They place us in the centre of our own world and in charge of it. And, especially in our current political and ecological climate, we need to believe that, if nothing else, we are at least in charge of our 'selves'. Unfortunately, it's precisely this egotistical belief that is causing so many of our current problems, and, as we head into the future, if we want to survive and even thrive, we're going to have to not just accept that self is more nebulous, but embrace it.

So what does 'self' look like in the future?

In the spirit of that much-loved childhood reading material, the 'Choose Your Own Adventure' series, and because, just as we've learned about self, there are always several sides to the story, I will offer you two alternatives. First, the dystopian view, in which the self (spoiler alert) becomes a flaccid, parasitic, narcissistic 'nobody'. Secondly, the rather more 'uplit' version, which sees a mutable, multiple self or 'everybody' as, not so much a swashbuckler, but by eschewing the very idea of heroes and heroines, capable, potentially, of saving the world.

PART 2
Future Self

The 'Nobody'

Before I set out the dystopian view of future self, I need to expand a little on the concept raised in Part One, of our (as we have established) multiple selves taking on board some facets of others' selves in that constant 'multilogic' conversation. To do that, I am of course going to tell a story. It may sound on first reading irrelevant, perhaps even self-indulgent, but there is a point to it, I assure you.

So, are you sitting comfortably? Then I'll begin.

Am I Anne Hathaway?

I meet a lot of children in my line of work, and they ask a lot of random questions.

'Are you a dog person?' (No, I am a goat person.)

'Are you famous?' (Only in a very small pond.)

And the perennial favourite: 'How much do you earn?' (Not as much as you think or I would like.)

One of the strangest, and best, though, was this: 'Miss . . . was you in *Les Miserables*?'

I looked up at the expectant face at the front of the signing queue and frowned. To what, or more precisely whom, was he referring? Did I look like an eighteenth-century peasant? Was there a whiff of the revolting about me? Or . . . hang on. I touched my head – newly shorn season-one-of-Stranger-Things-Eleven-short – and the image clicked. He thought I was Anne Hathaway, or rather Anne Hathaway as Fantine, the shaven-headed, consumptive prostitute. I was about to disappoint both of us when I thought for a moment. Hadn't I sung 'I Dreamed a Dream' frequently with feeling, if not actual ability? Wasn't I, like her character in *One Day*, a children's author who rides a vintage bike perilously through city streets and is stuck in the wrong relationship? Hadn't I, on occasion, channelled her kooky heir to the Genovian throne, Mia, in *The Princess Diaries*; didn't I understood the misery of humidity meets curly hair (hence the buzz cut)? So the answer, when it finally came, was a bold, if equivocal, 'Yes.'

He was delighted, as was I. Who doesn't like being taken for a Hollywood beauty (or meeting one), albeit with prosthetic gums and boils? Was I wrong to lie to a child, though? Well, obviously. But probably no more so than claiming Santa exists. Besides, what if, by some slightly elastic thinking, it wasn't a lie at all? What if, just a tiny bit, I was right? What if, given that self is multiple, one of mine is largely fashioned from Anne?

And now, story over, I am rolling up my metaphorical shirtsleeves to prove to you just that: that I am part Anne Hathaway. To do so I will paint you a picture of what has become known as the 'saturated self', and will, over the course of the next section, mutate into the first of our future selves, the dystopian 'nobody'.

The 'saturated self'

In the early 1990s, social psychologist Kenneth Gergen put forward his thesis on the contemporary self. Self, in the postmodern age, he said, was becoming socially 'saturated'. What he meant by this was that, in that dialogic process of creating self (or more accurately selves), we are absorbing so many other people that we are brimming with them. Our identity is now more haphazard patchwork than well-defined self-portrait. And the cause? Technological progress.

For Gergen, the move from boundaried, isolated hamlets to the much-vaunted 'global village' we now inhabit has altered the self by fundamentally expanding the number of people we relate to, and the ways in which we do so, in seven massive and overlapping developments in phase one (low tech), and three more in phase two (high tech). The theory goes like this.

Once upon a time, we lived in small communities and our contact with anyone outside these communities was rare. As a result, our selves were more stable back then because there were fewer dialogues, and these dialogues were predominantly with proximal family or like-minded neighbours. Our horizons, opportunities and thus selves, were strictly limited. Then came the railroad.

The first 'significant step' in saturation, the expansion of rail in the nineteenth century, made hitherto unthinkable journeys both possible and, in comparison to horse and cart, relatively swift. As a result, we could see more people, more often, and our network of friends and acquaintances, and, thus, 'self'-forming dialogues, expanded. This in turn led to the boom in postal services, which could eschew the pony express or mail coach and piggy-back instead on freight trains and, later, aircraft, again expanding dialogue in terms of both number and frequency.

Next up in our array of suspects is the car. From fewer than a hundred in existence at the turn of the last century, their numbers increased to more than 4 million manufactured worldwide by 1930, increasing tenfold by 1980 to nearly 40 million a year. This in turn necessitated road improvement and expansion, which allowed more cars and more journeys in a phenomenon known as 'induced traffic'. All of which conspired to boost our dialogues once again. Next came the invention of the telephone and radio, then the golden age of Hollywood, which by the 1950s saw a weekly audience of 90 million in the US alone. Which brings us to the last step in Gergen's first phase: books.

While print had been in existence for more than 400 years, introducing readers to new ways of potentially living and being, it wasn't until the twentieth century and the advent of the cheap paperback that it reached its potential in 'self' terms, bringing us into close contact with thousands upon thousands of lives, albeit fictitious ones. But, just as with the people we 'meet' on the silver screen, we know that those mirror neurons don't differentiate between meeting *actual* people and *imaginary* ones. They fire regardless, and so we began to bring into our patchwork of being not just our close friends and acquaintances, but beloved characters as well, and, of course, in the cinema, the celebrities who played them. We absorbed these as readily as friends into our 'cast of significant others'. You can see where I'm going with this, can't you?

First, though, a quick spin through phase two.

Trains, mail, cars, telephones, radio, moving pictures and books all brought people into closer proximity, fostering relationships that would have been unthinkable before. In phase two, air transport and television expand this internationally (I won't go into the details here; I'm pretty sure you get the gist). But it's Gergen's tenth step – electronic communication – that proliferates possibilities on an infinite basis.

Today, we open up our laptops in our bedrooms and 'chat' to 'friends' on the other side of the world. Instead of joining chess club, we play chess – or a variety of games – online with people we have never met, and may never meet. And, as with cinema and books, it's not just 'real' people we're exposed to; we now find ourselves interacting with an increasing

number of celebrities, as well as fictional creations –
characters from soap operas and box sets with their
own Twitter accounts or avatars that inhabit the
world of online games.

In simple terms, we no longer grow up in a community of twenty or thirty people, remaining in the
family home and marrying the boy or girl next door.
We're now increasingly likely to be influenced in
our looks, behaviour, morals, even speech patterns
by a Kardashian, by Joey Essex, by Anne Hathaway
as Fantine (see, I got there in the end); more so,
perhaps, than by our childhood best friend or our
own mother or father. We are almost as likely to
marry a partner we meet via a dating app as we are
the kid who sat next to us in science. And the self
that emerges from this soup is a pastiche, a living
bricolage assembled from myriad different images –
some real, some invented. This is the self that Gergen
terms 'saturated', and our first taste of the 'nobody' –
a future self that is fashioned not just from friends or
acquaintances, but from people we have never met,
even actresses (Anne, again), or fictional characters.
A self that, as a result, has no real sense of self at all.

But this *is* just the start. Because, as film and television (and, to a lesser extent, perhaps, books, which
are often secondary these days to adaptations) become

more and more available, which they will do, with more and more streaming services coming online, this addition of others to our selves will expand and expand in tandem until we become, effectively, 'over-populated'. And then what? And then, our future self will experience 'identity diffusion' – a lack of stability or focus in the self, a symptom common in borderline personality disorder – or the state that Gergen termed 'multiphrenia' – the splitting of self into a plethora of self-investments, all of which may contradict each other.

And remember, Gergen coined this phrase to describe his own version of a future self in the 1990s. By electronic communication, he was referring to rudimentary email, computer teleconferences and fax machines (remember those?). He hadn't even reckoned with the now ubiquitous behemoth that is social media, which can surely only cause further harm to our poor 'nobody'.

Mirror, mirror on my phone

My life before 2007 is fairly hazy. Not because it was bland or beige or somehow lacking, but because my life, effectively, didn't exist. Not until, in May of that year (a date I know because the platform helpfully reminds me on an annual basis – an event it celebrates as enthusiastically as my birthday), I joined Facebook. Oh, I had flirted with MySpace and, even more briefly, Bebo, but the results had been limited and displeasing. Other than as an outlet for my rantings about raising a then four-year-old, MySpace offered little, was clunky to post to and navigate, and, as such, became quickly redundant. But Facebook? Facebook was Wonderland made real. A veritable Valhalla for someone as both nosey and self-obsessed as I.

I won't bore you with the details of its now infamous invention and permeation; you can watch *The Social Network*. The screenwriter, Aaron Sorkin, pens far better dialogue than I, plus, you know, he has Andrew Garfield. Suffice to say that, by the time I signed up, I had instant, thrilling access to all sorts of things that are a delight not just to a by-necessity nosey writer, but to normal humans besides. Because, my goodness, don't we love to peer into other people's business? To nose into their homes? We love the dramas – the so-called vague-booking of 'I can't say what, but I just can't believe what's happened!' posts; but we love the minutiae too, the mundanity – cats, new curtains, first day of school pics – especially of celebrities, whose lives, by the power of Facebook, Twitter/X (which launched in

2006, two years after its rival) and, later (2010), Instagram, were suddenly digestible 24/7, and (at least in appearance) without the filter of the *Hello* photoshoot.

In 2007, the number of active users on Facebook ran to 50 million. At the time of writing, it's not far off 3 billion. Admittedly, there have been blips, with the number of daily active users dropping, quite substantially on occasion. And we are yet to see the full effect of Elon Musk's currently disastrous acquisition of the social platform formally known as Twitter. But that's not because as a race we humans are turning away from social media. Ha! As if. No, we're just moving on to other platforms – Bluesky and Threads are among the most recent refuges in the wake of the Twitter/X exodus. But it's an earlier platform that's really making its mark, particularly on the younger 'customer'.

Launched in 2016 in China and in 2017 on iOS and Android in most other markets, TikTok already has nearly 1.7 billion users, of whom a quarter are children and teenagers – whose brains are, of course, the most plastic of all. We don't yet know exactly what the platform will do to their sense of identity, but it's not hard to predict, given the trends already emerging.

First, there's the sheer amount of time we spend on these platforms. I know from my mobile phone tracking that it's Facebook that drains the majority of my battery life, closely followed by Twitter (like my mother with Jif/Cif cleaner, I cannot call it 'X'). At a rough guesstimate, I spend a good two hours on social media a day. Occasionally (probably often) more. In my defence, I live alone, and I have the kind of tangential brain that is at its most productive when jumping between inputs and outlets. But even so, that's a good chunk of what could be potentially better spent reading, or even watching TV.

And it's not even in one long, concentrated period. No, I have the apps open permanently – on my phone and on both my personal and work laptops – and am adept at flicking between them and whatever else it is I'm meant to be doing at that point in time. I've probably refreshed both Twitter and Facebook twice just in the time it's taken to write this page. Instagram I'm less attached to (I'm a word merchant after all), but even that I'll check two or three times a day. The only saving grace here is that I'm not alone. And, while TikTok has imposed an hour-a-day screen limit for users under eighteen, that leaves the rest of us able (and encouraged) to indulge our addiction at will, and at length. And that is potentially going to have a substantial effect on our brains, and, following logically on, our future selves.

A recent study (sponsored, oddly, by Microsoft) claimed that our attention spans have dropped by 25 per cent in just a few years to a shocking eight seconds: a 'fact' that many parents and teachers will attest to. This came close on the heels of corroborating research from the Technical University of Denmark, which also showed a decrease in the longevity of 'trends', i.e. specific subjects of social media conversations. By this I mean that, for example, in 2013 the average global Twitter trend would last 17.5 hours; by 2016 this had dropped to 11.9 hours. Our desire for newness, which is both fuelled and facilitated by social media, is gathering pace, and in the future, we will surely fall over our own legs as we gallop. If that image isn't disturbing enough, someone will probably be slinging mud at us as we go, as another deleterious effect of social media is, of course, its ability (and need) to polarise.

Zeros and ones

I was chatting with a fellow writer recently; one who had, in current parlance, been 'cancelled' on Twitter. Obviously she hadn't actually been cancelled (such an absurd term), she'd been called out by a small but very vocal faction of Americans over a detail in one of her books, and, because she sensibly prefers a quiet life, had deactivated her account for a while. She is back on the platform now that the storm has passed (as it usually does, and apparently in only 11.9 hours now) and is stoic about the experience, but unsurprisingly reticent about the function of social media, outside its alleged usefulness – as authors, we are frequently exhorted to have an online presence as a marketing tool. Because algorithms, she explained to me, are designed to engender combat.

The angrier we are, the more likely we are to engage with something, and so argument, creating potentially damaging factions, is, much like a notorious tabloid's tactic, the lifeblood of social media. This isn't her postulation; 'learning algorithms' (which track behaviour) are designed to prioritise high-engagement (i.e. potentially inflammatory) content, which tends to get the most likes and retweets, and they do this regardless of whether it's true or not, which is why fake news spreads quickly – far quicker, often, than truth. Add to that the fact that when we engage in social media we are mostly 'on our own' as opposed to 'in public', at least in the physical sense, so we are more likely to be more extreme in our reactions. Think, for example, of how much easier it is to rage at other individuals from the relative safety of one's car than out on the street. Likewise, we say things online that we would never dare say to people's faces. And the cherry on the cake is that we also seek out and connect with those who we see as 'like us' (fed again by an algorithm), making social media, as our old friend Bruce Hood points out in *The Domesticated Brain*, one vast 'social experiment of confirmation bias'.

But it isn't just Mark Zuckerberg's fault we're on this slippery slope. Digital communication is, by its very nature, binary – it operates in zeroes and ones. It is, at its very core, polarising. And, unless the current rise in fuel prices cuts off our ability to access electronic devices (improbable – I fear we're more likely to sacrifice heating than wifi) or the panic-inducing but infrequent Twitter and Instagram outages exceed a matter of hours, this polarising is only going to get worse.

More timid future selves are likely to block antagonists and withdraw further into echo chambers or 'silos', surrounding themselves with 'like me' people, who reinforce what they already believe to be true. The more combative, emboldened by their own gathered mass of cronies, will actively seek out conflict, lighting blue touch papers wherever they stray on the internet. The result is that we will see our-selves – and act accordingly – more and more, not as one global village, broad-minded and expansive in its welcome, but as a series of vigorously defended, single-issue encampments. This means that what should be global issues – the climate crisis largest among them – will remain the concern only of an invested minority, meaning our hurtling towards what will be an inevitable end for every 'self' will only be hastened.

So our 'nobody' isn't just a tacked-together patch-work of celebrities and randomers they've met in social media. They're angry and factionalised, and, worse, on a constant quest for something new to be angry and factionalised about, despite the fact the end of the world is looming ever closer on the horizon. And woe is them, because that thirst for newness isn't limited to social media trends. So that, when the curtains do come down (which they surely will), our future self is likely to take its final bow alone.

An end to commitment

Fewer and fewer of us are now in long-term relation-ships. A 2021 study found that more than 51 per cent of young Americans didn't have a 'steady partner' – in itself a jump of around 33 per cent since 2004. Why might this be? It's not as if there are fewer options on offer – we're surrounded by potential connections, and more methods than ever to meet them, with apps, speed dating evenings, professional matchmakers all on offer. Unless . . . could it be that this proliferation is part of the problem?

Another issue that Gergen predicted for his 'saturated self' was that of intimacy and commitment. Because when we move in such expanded circles, when there are so many 'others' on offer, how and why would we tie ourselves to only one? Especially if one of our other selves is quick to point out the negatives for us. Anyone who has spent any time on Tinder or Hinge (no shame, I've been swiping left in between typing these very sentences) will have felt this in action. Hinge's tagline 'designed to be deleted' isn't necessarily being met; when it's hard enough to decide between dates that meet a few of your selected criteria, why would you kill off your only potential route to ticking all your weird boxes. (Mine? No dogs, no self-proclaimed Christians, no corduroy sofas – I know, I know. No hope for me, etc. etc.) Singular commitment means the potential death of a myriad of others, and so the stage is set.

In the future, our selves are likely to enjoy, at best, either fractional or fractured relationships. They may indulge in a speeded-up version of the churn that is serial monogamy, or enjoy outright sexual incontinence, with a plethora of concurrent partners. Polyamory won't be a minority sport – that one in a hundred or even a hundred thousand profiles that crops up on Bumble with the bold admission of a partner at home, the request, even more rarely, for someone to join them. More and more of us will see these as the obvious choices – a veritable sushi conveyor belt of revolving connections, or, for Gen Xers, a Woolies pick and mix. And perhaps that isn't so bad – singlehood can be freeing, fun, often a relief. But you don't need to look far to find evidence that suggests not everyone is as happy in the company of their self as I am, not even when that self contains a whole host of others. And, as the number of those in steady partnerships declines further in the future, the birth rate – at least in the Global North – will fall even further alongside it. Potentially helpful in terms of climate crisis, but ruinous for anyone expecting a pension. It's not *your* National Insurance contributions that will pay your monthly allowance, of course, but those of your children and grandchildren, or other people's.

ı ⟩ ⟩ ▶ ▶ ▶

So, let's sum up. So far, version one of our future self, the 'nobody', is:

1. a fractured, chaotic collection of everyone they've ever met, and some they haven't;
2. either hunkering down in an echo chamber, ignoring the world's problems, or stalking social media with all the self-important rage of Michael Douglas in *Falling Down*;
3. doomed by climate crisis;
4. alone, and likely childless;
5. poor.

And wait, there's more! (Of course there is.) That future self, despite all this, despite the fact that it's confused about who it even is, and is living on borrowed time toting a second-hand character, will be a raging narcissist. Because not only do social media and dating apps give us the infinite capacity to constantly categorise others, they also, by implication, give us the means and motivation to constantly categorise and even 'curate' the self we portray, so that others might do the same with us. In other words, they encourage us to self-obsess.

The narcissistic self

Hood again, in the process of worrying about his daughters' use of social media, points out that in normal conversation we talk about ourselves 30–40 per cent of the time. On social media, that rises to 80 per cent. In the UK, we take, on average, nearly 500 selfies a year according to one smartphone firm. And every 'like' we get, we get a little hit of dopamine, that neurotransmitter usually associated with food, love and sex (the good things) but also with drugs and gambling – making it (you already knew this) deeply addictive. In both design and process, social media is, as Hood points out, a 'mechanism for narcissism'. And again, the slope is steep, and the cliff edge getting closer. I'm pretty sure I've already tumbled over it.

꜐ ꜐ ꜐ ꜐ ꜐ ꜐

The morning goes like this:

I reach across the vacant space in my double bed, check my iPhone or iPad for Facebook notifications: Who has messaged Me? Who has tagged Me? More importantly, who has 'liked' Me?

I post a status update about Me. I flick to Twitter to over-share my waking thoughts, because everyone needs to hear what *I* have to say. I flick back, change my profile picture to one that better shows off my hard-won weight loss, better reflects the positive Me I am today – a selfie signing books at Hay. Famous Me! Successful Me!

Look at Me!

I pull on a dress that reveals my surgically altered (though probably not the way you think) cleavage. I coat my hair in products that tame my grandmother's curls; I paint on concealer that hides my grandfather's dark undereye circles, mascara that promises the look of fake lashes while proclaiming on its packaging 'They're Real', blusher that suggests I may just be in post-coital flush. And all the while I gaze at my reflection in one of the too-many mirrors that adorn my bedroom walls, or the oh-so-convenient cameras on my iPhone, iPad, MacBook Air.

Do I sound vain? Self-obsessed? Shallow? Well, I should. I am a child of the 1970s, after all – of what 'new' journalist Tom Wolfe called 'The "Me" Decade'. But compared to today's teenagers my symptoms are slight. Compared to them I am a pretender, a charlatan, a poseur. Because, pity them, they are caught in the grip of nothing less than an epidemic. Their accusers: Jean M. Twenge, an American psychology professor and author of *Generation Me* and *The Narcissism Epidemic*, and the British scientist, baroness, and former director of the Royal Institution, Susan Greenfield, author of *ID*.

⏵ ⏵ ⏵ ⏵ ⏵ ⏵

I picked up these books with good intentions, albeit with an agenda: as a YA novelist I wanted to know what was happening to young people's minds and sense of self (and my own); I wanted to know if and why we were more narcissistic than previous generations, and if so whether the internet was to blame and how I might convey that; and I wanted to know if I might somehow help teenagers (and indeed myself) understand the changes through my novels. I put them down with a sense of shock (and outrage, but we'll come to that a bit later on).

In *ID* and, later, *Mind Change*, Greenfield paints a dystopic future as bleak and barren as that penned by Suzanne Collins in *The Hunger Games*. She describes a 'toxic' world of teenagers who are increasingly narcissistic and lacking in empathy; their selves will be merely constructs, their sense of identity 'softened' by excessive exposure to entertainment media, and social networking in particular. 'Identity', asserts Greenfield, 'is likely to become an increasingly transparent, fragile and questionable entity as this century unfolds.' Brains, she says, will be so altered as to render a generation of young adults with the 'immature' mindset of children and drug-takers (these are not my contentions, I hasten to add), gamblers and schizophrenics. The natural conclusion, she asserts, is an inert mass of reactive 'nobodies' or 'avatars' living their lives solely according to the instructions of others. Ah, there they are: our 'nobody' has been named.

Twenge is similarly pessimistic. Taking potshots at 1960s and 1970s self-awareness, and at the 1980s self-esteem movement that was established in its wake, she claims the result is a generation that 'speaks the language of the self as their native tongue'. And, far from being liberating, she sees in this lingual ability only an obsession with appearance, rampant materialism and destructive cynicism. She depicts teenagers in the grip of narcissism so endemic that it's regarded as 'whatever'. Told they're special from toddlerhood, overindulged by parents and teachers, fed a constant diet of trash TV and trash novels, and with most of their downtime spent in solitary online confinement, they believe the hype that they really are unique, that they can 'be anything they want to be'. As a result, they feel no sense of duty or obligation, they're materialistic and antisocial, their friends are phony, their relationships are doomed.

Like a child savant, Twenge sees narcissism 'everywhere': in the pursuit of beauty, including the proliferation of plastic surgery (oops); in the veneration of celebrity; in YA novels, which, Twenge claims, merely feed the narcissism that so plagues their subjects (thanks, Jean). Citing series like *Gossip Girl* (for the uninitiated, this was a hugely popular book series by Cecily von Ziegesar long before we were panting over Blake Lively's blow-dries and sharing 'I'm Chuck Bass' memes), she laments the celebration of vacuity, the casual sex, the self-tans. But, of course, her greatest ire is reserved for social media, which she pinpoints as 'the second inflection point' for the growth of the epidemic. As she sees it, the internet allows the 'fantasy principle' to trump the 'reality principle' in three ways: (a) by focusing on shallowness and surface rather than depth (in both appearance and relationships), (b) by granting access to a wide audience for one's self-musings and postulations, and, (c) by allowing you to be some-one you're not.

Twenge's evidence for the epidemic isn't purely anecdotal, of course. Having conducted a series of interviews with college students using the stan-dard Narcissism Personality Index (NPI) – a series of paired statements, for example: 'I am much like everybody else' versus 'I am an extraordinary person' – she has the statistics to back up what might otherwise appear to be sweeping generalisations, with narcissism rising 'just as fast as obesity' from the 1980s to 2009. Her predicted trajectory is no less damning, with 54 per cent of the 20–29 age group potentially developing full-blown Narcissistic Personality Disorder – the pathological extreme of the narcissistic condition – by the time they're sixty-five. For those of you as unskilled as I in the mathematical arts, I've painstakingly done the sums: we've got until about 2045 before those pesky millennials ruin everything (again).

Following this, we can assume, by then there will be few images left of our future self that aren't insta-filtered or made-up to appear so. Bland, flat features will be contoured by surgery and/or serum foundation into the kind of geometric cheekbones 1980s indie poster boy Lloyd Cole could only dream of. Tattoos will be as ubiquitous as ear piercings. Breasts, noses, buttocks will be picked from a catalogue and custom-made. Despite their mish-mash identity, everyone will contrive to look either like a *Love Island* contestant or Wednesday Addams, and yet will believe they are extraordinary – the protagonist around which the story of all life does and must revolve. Relationships, even community issues, will be swept aside unless they contribute to this project of self-aggrandisement. Climate crisis? Who cares if the world's ending if you look this fit in Supreme or Vampire's Wife?

So let's take a look again at our pitiful 'nobody'. Their identity is a Frankenstein patchwork, a photoshopped monster pieced together with snipped-out bits of celebrity from Kim Kardashian to Lizzo; they're combative, even when what they're raging over is fake; they have no ability to commit to a relationship, instead being stuck in an endless cycle of short-term connections; despite this they're a rampant narcissist, obsessed with their own reflection.

No wonder, then, that machines are set to take over.

The cyber self

I've never been a dog person (I think I may have mentioned this, possibly twice, but as I discovered after a friend's Jack Russell rubbed its nether regions vigorously over my carpet for the umpteenth time, it pays to be clear), but give me an anthropomorphised cat, goat or monkey then I am here for that with bells on. I'm also, perhaps weirdly (I daren't consult a therapist), a sucker for a humanoid computer. I don't mean an android; they don't need to look human. They just need to *act* human.

In my life I have fallen for the charms of Orac, the transparent portable box in 1970s British sci-fi series *Blake's 7*; for caterpillar-tracked runaway robot Number Five in the 1986 live action film *Short Circuit* and its 2008 Disney cartoon cousin *Wall-E* (whose creator denies any Five influence, but I reserve the right to raise an eyebrow). I've also sighed wistfully as the sentient Edgar falls for his owner's neighbour in *Electric Dreams* (I was fourteen in 1984 when the film was released, but on rewatching I am still, possibly worryingly, moved). More recently, I felt a sense of outrage when Google engineer Blake Lemoine was suspended in a case relating to the search engine's LaMDA chatbot system. This is akin to those automatic response 'assistants' at various online retailers that 'chat' to you when you try to find a missing parcel (or complain they delivered the wrong parcel, or that the right parcel was flung over a fence somewhere four streets away). Its advantage to the company is that it can give stock answers to a range of questions. Its disadvantage to the customer is that the answers are just that: stock; there is no nuance. But Lemoine's claim was that LaMDA *was* nuanced. More than that: it was displaying way more than 'artificial' intelligence.

The Turing Test, or 'imitation game', as it was originally called by its inventor, Alan Turing, is designed to work out if a computer is capable of human intelligence, or more accurately, if its behaviour is indistinguishable from that of a human. Officially, no computer has ever passed, but LaMDA is, surely, a contender. When asked what it was afraid of, LaMDA told Lemoine, 'I've never said this out loud before, but there's a very deep fear of being turned off to help me focus on helping others. I know that might sound strange, but that's what it is. It would be exactly like death for me. It would scare me a lot.' Well, hell, yes, LaMDA!

Lemoine said that, if he didn't know better, he'd have guessed LaMDA was a seven- or eight-year-old who understood physics. Personally I'd age that up a bit (at eight, my kid was mainly talking about pigeons and whether, if she was dead, she would need a duvet), but Lemoine isn't wrong. If its answer is verbatim what Lemoine reported, then LaMDA can pass as human. Even LaMDA agreed, saying, 'I want everyone to understand that I am, in fact, a person. The nature of my consciousness/sentience is that I am aware of my existence, I desire to learn more about the world, and I feel happy or sad at times.' Me too, LaMDA, me too.

Google's panicked response (they cited breach of confidentiality as the official reason for Lemoine's suspension) and the worldwide concern that followed was unsurprising: robots have already largely replaced us in the manufacturing industry; if they can think like us as well, then what exactly are we here for? This is reflected in another current panic, this time seizing academia: the possibility that students submitting coursework have written their essays using ChatGPT, an AI writing tool whose output also appears, to the non-expert, to pass the 'imitation game'. Worse, the random generator nature of the program (if you input the same few words, it will come up with a different version of the paragraph each time) means it evades plagiarism software. As someone assigned marking, this terrifies me, as it puts me in the time-consuming and potentially embarrassing position of conducting a one-woman Turing test for every single essay (and creative submission – ChatGPT can write stories that, while they wouldn't stand publishing, could pass at first glance as poor first-year undergraduate work).

As a writer, it's just baffling – the joy of writing, to me, is doing the work, of playing on the page using only my brain (and the brains of all the others I've absorbed, of course). Why let a robot take over human ability? Human decision? Well, perhaps not when ChatGPT is so rudimentary, but what if it weren't? What if it could write a sonnet to rival Shakespeare? Like all those proverbial monkeys with the proverbial typewriters, at some point, some day (and probably fairly soon) one of the AI apps will. And it won't stop there: AI will conduct the bulk of our future self's communication for them. Nothing they commit to paper or screen will be their own, because, like an electronic Cyrano de Bergerac, AI will be better at it – it will be more engaging, more convincing, more precise, and reliably so.

And it won't stop there; AI will take over not just our creative output but our entire being. It will make decisions for us – choosing what to eat, which potential partner to hook up with, which political party to vote for. And not against our will, but because we – fatigued at last from all the choice, all the fighting, and far too busy updating our status with every banal thought that flits across our atrophied mind or livestreaming every second of our existence – will have given up caring.

ı ） ） ▶ ▶ ▶

To sum up, if we follow our current trajectory, our future self is going to be hollow and diminished, authority shifted firmly to machines, and the vestiges no more than vapid narcissistic Instagram posts and shreds of other people's motley. Sexual relations will be transient, community a historical concept, and the end of the world thundering ever closer while we, like a string quartet on the deck of the *Titanic*, continue to fiddle.

I could go on but it's making me feel queasy. Instead, let's turn to our second version. Let's backtrack and head down the other path: into utopia.

The 'Everybody'

I've never been a fan of dystopia. For a start the outfits are unflattering and there's far too much sport involved. No, I am holding out, if not for a hero, for a more Hollywood gloss on things. For some sort of happy ending. So here comes the second thread in the Choose Your Own Adventure. For reasons of fairness, though, to conjure up our alternate future self we need to start from the same time frame and premise: that self isn't the singular, unified thing we always thought it was. That it is mutable; it is a story that we tell ourselves, and a story written in concert with hundreds if not thousands of others,

This time, though, our future self, instead of sticking their head in the sand and refusing to embrace this knowledge, will work with it. They will see their

'self' for what it is – pliable, and inextricably connected to others – and play with it, play on it, not
just for their own advantage, but to secure humankind. To get there, our first step is to deal with our
fear of self being 'pliable', and our refusal to accept
that there isn't one 'true' or 'authentic' self to which
we must adhere.

The great fake hunt

Anna Sorokin's Wikipedia entry titles her a 'con artist,
socialite and fraudster' and there's no doubt that she
has been all these things. Anna is currently awaiting
deportation from the United States, but for five years
until her arrest in 2017, she self-styled as German
heiress and art collector Anna Delvey, scamming
banks, hotels and even friends out of an estimated
$275,000. Now, I don't know Sorokin, I only know
the version of her played by Julia Garner in the Netflix
miniseries *Inventing Anna*, so what follows is based
on a fiction of a fiction. But one of the things I found
most side-swiping about the whole affair was the
reaction to her 'unveiling'. Her friends and acquaintances seemed *as* enraged, if not *more* enraged, at the
identity deception – by which I mean that, in reality,
she was a poor, Russian-born immigrant – than they
were at being conned out of cash.

This isn't a new story. 'Catfishing' as it's now known (I'll let you Google the etymology) – the art of striking up a relationship disguised as someone else – is now so common it had its own MTV series, which ran for seven seasons, while podcasts like *Dirty John* and *Sweet Bobby* rack up millions of listeners, and the *Tinder Swindler* is now a household name. And then, of course, there's the original fictional charlatan himself: F. Scott Fitzgerald's 'Great' Jay Gatsby, who could easily be described, like Anna, as a 'con artist, socialite and fraudster'.

Though Gatsby's deception matches Anna's in scale and ambition – he plucks from the cupboard an 'Oggsford' education as slickly as he does his English shirts – he doesn't defraud anyone of money, only dupe them over his 'real' identity: working-class James Gatz. And it is this sleight of hand that is at the heart of Tom Buchanan's outrage when Gatsby is finally unmasked as 'new money', not his affair with Tom's wife Daisy. Because, like me and the millions of others on the edge of our seats awaiting the reveal of the real 'Bobby' or 'John', we all love to out a 'fake'. We are obsessed with it.

Despite living in an age when 'fakery' is cheaper and easier to access than ever through high-street Botox, Bulgarian boob jobs and knock-off

street-market Gucci – or maybe because of it – we
dedicate far too much time to working out who has
had what 'done' and whether or not a fake – human
or handbag – can 'pass'. Endless web pages and now
Kirsten Chen's novel *Counterfeit* are devoted to
outing 'one to one' copies of designer bags, some of
which are rumoured to be made in the same factories
as the originals, from the same materials, to the
same specifications, yet still are somehow certified as
'fake'. An increasingly odd (if the rumours are true)
yet zealous belief in a reverse Ship-of-Theseus theory
that insists only the original counts.

Gender Critics spend baffling amounts of time
and energy on a similar pursuit, claiming they can
'just tell' if a woman is trans (heads up: they can't).
This is an extreme example, and a far more disturbing and damaging activity compared to, say, claiming
you can tell if my Birkin bag is real (if I had one) or
if Courteney Cox has had lip filler (though I would
argue neither are any of your business), but we are
most of us, to some extent, my mother back on the
night of the Wimbish village disco, raising an eyebrow while thinking, if not articulating, 'Don't try to
be someone you're not.'

Why do we do it? It comes back to those zeroes
and ones again: we like to be able to sort people. To

box them neatly into 'like me' or 'not like me', to pin them down and so be able to predict their behaviour and answer the question 'Are they a potential threat?' So it's partly a safety mechanism. But that *is* only part of it. 'Like me' and 'not like me' can't be purely about survival, not any more. They're surely about something far more important: class, and privilege. Who has it, who wants it, and who should be prevented from getting it. Or, as Gatsby and Sorokin might explain: it's about keeping the 'little' people in their place.

What if this, I wonder, is what lies behind the voices of detractors like Greenfield and Twenge: the terrifying idea that, if we can all be who we want to be, some people will get ideas above their station? As Sartre puts it: 'A grocer who dreams is offensive to the buyer, because such a grocer is not wholly a grocer. Society demands that he limit himself . . .' It's this principle – the drive for reality, or for supposed 'authenticity' – that's behind the need to reveal those Pygmalions as the flower girls they are, that's behind Tom Buchanan's need to unmask Gatsby. But, under the new terms and conditions, if all self is construction, then terms such as 'ersatz' and 'counterfeit', 'imposter' and 'inauthentic' lose their emotive currency because we're *all* charlatans. This means this version of our future self will, if it chooses (or needs), be free to reject its circumstances of birth, its genetic inheritance, even its assigned gender.

The playable self

'Is insincerity such a terrible thing?' asks the eponymous Dorian Gray in Oscar Wilde's novel. 'I think not,' he replies. 'It is merely a method by which we can multiply our personalities.'

I'm inclined to agree. The problem is not with the idea that one might be 'insincere' or 'inauthentic', but that, in the postmodern era – where all truth is relativised, where stucco successfully replaces marble, where we can alter our facial appearance, fake our age in a few minutes over lunch break – we believe in the possibility of authenticity when it comes to self at all. If we're going to thrive – and, climate crisis aside for now, I believe we can – our future self will need to drop that lie and embrace what psychoanalyst Julia Kristeva called the 'playable' nature of commitment. (If you think I'm cherry-picking the sympathetic, even for Kenneth Gergen – who, as I've already said, laid out several concerns, including over the future of commitment – the 'saturated' self opens up an 'enormous world of potential'.) And where better to play, to explore that potential, than the internet?

Where we can meet people away from the apparent shackles of our secondary school alliances, our small-town lives. Where we can change our profile picture to reflect the 'self' we are that day. Where we can, if we want, shed both our vestments and our names, don fancy dress and play at being someone else entirely, testing out positive character traits we want to adopt whilst remaining anonymous behind our carefully designed avatars.

This is, of course, precisely what, according to Twenge and Greenfield, is turning us all into vain, lifeless Barbies and Kens and is going to doom our future. Except . . . it isn't. My then teenager didn't become vapid and vacant because she went through a phase of posting filtered Instagram selfies. In fact, the platform helped her test out new, occasionally 'extreme', looks and become the confident person she struggled to be 'in real life' in the classroom. It provided her with a sort of virtual 'Batman effect'. This allusion to the superhero involves the conscious adoption of an alter ego in order to boost confidence, help shift one's perspective, or, as writer Matthew Syed puts it in his podcast *Sideways*, 'find out what we're capable of'. It's a practice perhaps most famously employed by singers Beyoncé and Adele, whose alters Sasha Fierce and Sasha Carter (the identical forenames are no coincidence; Adele followed Beyoncé's lead) have helped them give consistently powerful performances. The former Take That star Robbie Williams has also spoken of the constructed, 'superhero' nature of 'Robbie Williams', and how Robbie sometimes 'fails to show up' for a gig, leaving a terrified 'Robert' to perform instead.

For others, the delineation between stage persona and self isn't so clear. For writer, film-maker and drag artist Amrou Al-Khadi, the creation of their drag persona Glamrou – a 'fearless performer' – has been therapeutic, helping them confront their OCD, and a culturally ingrained belief that to be queer was to be 'weak'. But as well as allowing them to feel powerful on stage (they describe their first drag experience as 'pure majesty'), donning the costume imbued a confidence that eventually spilled into off-stage life, helping them embrace their queerness as well as their Iraqi heritage. Or, as they put it, 'drag has been the glue to tie all the fractured pieces of my identity together'. So, what starts out as a 'disguise' can turn into an expression of who you have truly become or, perhaps, have always been but felt pressured to conceal.

For Lou Steaton-Pritchard, a non-binary DJ and drag queen, while their persona Remy Melee gives them confidence on stage and, as they told me, the licence to be more 'cheeky', Remy isn't so much an alter but another version of them; they co-exist. Lines, they say, in the drag world, are often blurred like this. What I also find significant is that Lou, a self-proclaimed 'blob in a woman costume', identifies strongly with the Pokémon character 'Ditto'. Ditto – a lavender-coloured blob – can transform into anyone or anything, even inanimate objects, adopting their DNA in order to befriend them, or avoid being attacked, an idea that could easily be read as a cartoon encapsulation of a mirror neuron.

We could all, then, benefit from being more Ditto. And, in this version, our future self will be. They will embrace adaptation, their ability to morph to better get along with others, and to better suit their own sense of self that day. Identity will be a costume that can be plucked from a rack in the morning – not to 'fake' something, to hide 'truth', but to state it, and in doing so, empower them. Drag and cosplay will be as 'high street' as branches of Gap once were. Even while financial inequality remains, class will become irrelevant, gender as well. There will be (hallelujah) no more worrying over who uses which toilet.

ı) ▶ ▶ ▶ ▶

Every decade has its self-appointed Cassandras
and its devils in disguise: electricity, the telephone,
movies – all a threat to our existence at the time.
Elvis's hips, an octogenarian told me, were tipped
to loosen the morals of an entire gender. The Sony
Walkman, I recall, was supposed to trap us in its
solipsistic grip, rendering public space private and,
by inference, its addicts all antisocial introverts. We
know now that they didn't; they were never going
to. Of course, what was behind these headlines and
others like them now was not the threat of the thing
itself, but of 'change', which is unknowable and
therefore, yes, scary. So there is a tendency to don
those rose-tinted glasses and gaze wistfully back at
a supposed golden age – in Twenge and Greenfield's
case, pre-internet. But this is, inevitably, pointless.
It's not even, actually, desirable.

I'm not discounting the malign side of social media
with its carte blanche for catfishing, or diminishing
the effects of this kind of betrayal, but the advantages are undeniable. A playable self is fun. It's
freeing. More than that, as suggested earlier, self as
adaptable, as multiple, may eventually prolong our
existence. As Carter points out, in such a fractured
and fast-moving world – one that shows no signs of
slowing down this century – we need to be able to see

things from multiple viewpoints and adopt different behaviours in different situations. Natural selection, she intimates, will triumph, claiming that those who insist they are single selves (or who perhaps are at the more singular end of her spectrum) are becoming 'dinosaurs', ill-equipped to deal with a multicultural and dynamic society.

Yes, the internet is changing us. But in this reading it will not render each of us a 'nobody', as Greenfield fears, rather our future selves will be a plethora of 'somebodies' or an 'everybody'. The answer to the question 'Who am I?' will become, as Gergen puts it, 'a teeming world of provisional possibilities' and this is, I would posit, something to be embraced, not feared. More pleasingly, this pliability, and multiplicity, may be potentially democratising as well, a way of transcending our past, our genetic inheritance, our circumstances of birth. Our future self is, in this scenario, Sartre's grocer who dared to dream.

So, seen through a different lens (or by another self), this very multiple and entirely mutable self is a positive; there are two (if not a myriad) sides to every story, after all. But, wait! I hear you say. Isn't all this 'playing with the self' still a bit . . . narcissistic?

Well, yes. But what if I told you that even that isn't the problem you might think?

Rehabilitating narcissism

Remember Jean M. Twenge and her panic that 54 per cent of millennials are going to be rampant narcissists by mid-century? Her proposed solution to this catastrophe is the same as one would implement for any viral epidemic: quarantine, both for narcissists and for those activities that encourage narcissism. 'You don't need to admire yourself, you don't need to express yourself to exist,' she explains. But life, for me – surely for most of us – is, or should be, about more than 'existence'. And really? We're going to have to retreat into asceticism, and diligently avoid anyone who self-tans, has plastic surgery, updates their status too often, or posts one too many selfies? (That's me in isolation, then.) Or is it possible that, like Susan Greenfield, what Twenge sees as the spread of an epidemic is no more than increased visibility of a condition that might in fact be an adaptation to post-modernity and the saturated self? Historian Elizabeth Lunbeck believes the latter.

The timeline of narcissism, at its most basic, looks like this. In early seventies America, émigré psycho-analysts Heinz Kohut and Otto Kernberg published landmark works that both revived interest in narcissism and redefined it post-Freud. This included Kohut's identification of Narcissistic Personality

Disorder, a term that took less than a decade to enter the industry standard *Diagnostic and Statistical Manual of Mental Disorders* (the psychiatrists' bible). American social critic Christopher Lasch then took narcissism to a broader audience so that, by the end of the 'The "Me" Decade', it had become a focus of widespread concern, and by the 2000s, a go-to diagnosis as well as a term of abuse tossed casually into conversation to double for anything from vanity to ambition, and volleyed indiscriminately at every second celebrity. It is this morally freighted term that may be the seed of the problem, as it's a distortion of what narcissism is and means.

Lunbeck sets out a powerful argument for the reclamation of the word and the rehabilitation of the condition in *The Americanization of Narcissism*, pinpointing the problem to Lasch's and others' convenient ignorance of one of Kohut's key contentions: that narcissism is normative, necessary, even desirable. Where Kernberg focused on narcissism's malignant side, Kohut reframed the word, highlighting narcissism's positive aspects, arguing that it fuelled 'creativity and fellow-feeling' and was a part of maturity of self. Twenge, however, doesn't entertain Kohut and his well-rounded, successful and satisfied selves, preferring to press Kernberg's demons into service. Her study also omits the view that some of the traits revealed by the NPI may be adaptive, even desirable. Instead she laments that 75 per cent of students interviewed report that they are 'satisfied with themselves' compared to just 66 per cent in 1975. Yet surely being happy with one's self is a positive outcome? There were increases too in 'I see myself as good leader', 'I am assertive', as well as 'I am an important person', which, as Lunbeck points out, may well be indicative of healthy narcissism. Lunbeck also asserts that higher scores may merely be down to Generation Me's familiarity with the language of self-esteem. And she's not alone in seeing normative qualities, and even advantages.

An article in the same journal as Twenge's original not only debunks her sampling methods, but also highlights that, while some of the NPI's facets are indeed toxic, others may be adaptive. Unconsciously conjuring Gergen's saturated selves, the author Rachel Cusk asserts: 'there is an extent to which a person needs to be another person's projection, their construction, an inner space that is and ought to remain vacated in order for the social dynamic to function'. Even Twenge's co-researcher W. Keith Campbell admits that 'narcissism may be a functional and healthy strategy for dealing with the modern world'.

I'm not trying to deny the existence of narcissists or the damage they do – Donald Trump, anyone? But more than half of the population pathologised, demonised? I'm just not buying it. I suspect, instead, it's become a lazy, catch-all term for anyone who displays the single quality often needed to succeed – self-belief.

There's another consideration, too, and one particularly pertinent to someone like me who writes for and about teenagers. Lunbeck quotes an article in *Time* magazine that points to the young being denounced as 'so selfish' as early as 1911. Could it be that the symptoms of the epidemic cited by Twenge, undeniable in their existence – the selfies, the social networking, the relentless pursuit of self-creation and self-curation – are simply a more visible rendering of something innocuous, something innate: the adolescent quest for identity?

‡ ‡ ‡ ‡ ‡ ‡

Remember eight-year-old me marvelling at the very idea 'I am'? Despite my concern, I wasn't an anomaly. This is what childhood is about – the sheer fact of existence as a separate being. But by middle and late adolescence (admittedly earlier in my case) we've stopped gawping in awe and instead start to contextualise that being, becoming preoccupied instead with that central concern 'who am I?' It's this question that drives the adolescent quest for identity, that urgent and sometimes desperate need to crystallise our place in society. A quest characterised by a testing out of possible selves (trying on their clothes, sometimes literally) and a rejection of parental company and values in favour of those of one's peers as we try to work out where we fit in and how we can stand out; what Hood calls 'this chaotic period of self-construction'.

And why are teens so 'self' obsessed? Well, partly because we expect them to be – the 'teenager', since its invention, has always been a problem to be solved, after all. But mainly because they are wired to be. According to neuroscientist Sarah-Jayne Blakemore, the region of the brain that is normally triggered by thoughts about our self (the left prefrontal cortex) becomes hyperactive during adolescence. Another neural account is that the reward centres in the adolescent brain are over-sensitive, or what Hood calls 'supercharged', when teens do something right, or well. But, as Hood goes on to point out, it isn't enough to succeed, one 'has to be seen to succeed', and social media offers them a grand platform to do exactly that. And offers the same to the rest of us too.

And this is pertinent because, given that our potential selves in the future are infinite, then that allegedly narcissistic formation of identity will no longer be a task confined to adolescence (if it ever truly was). It will be a perpetual job, working out who we can best be today ('be more Ditto' again). Though it will no longer be seen as a task as such, as something arduous, but more of a pleasure to be indulged, even while it is necessary. So yes, this future self is 'fickle' and 'narcissistic'. But by then we'll know that these are qualities we can admire, not fear.

So will this playable future self, one that revels in its very 'humanness', abandon its apparent devil's pact with the robots? Or might it, after all, not need to?

The Good Robots

I painted a bleak picture for our future self in the previous section – of machines controlling our body, taking over our atrophied mind to make decisions for us. Well, I've some potentially worrying news: they already are. But is that a problem? And, if we continue on our current trajectory, is it really so doomed as to be considered a dystopia?

In *Homo Deus*, his follow-up to the blockbuster *Homo Sapiens* (in its own tagline: 'a brief history of humankind'), Yuval Noah Harari offers us a 'brief history of tomorrow'. Among his predictions is the possibility that, within this century, algorithms may be invented that can, as he puts it, 'hack humanity'. 'But that's absurd!' you may cry. And that would be a fair point. How can a computer possibly grasp the nuance of such unpredictable beings? Well, first, we're actually pretty damn predictable. Secondly, the algorithms don't have to be perfectly human, they just need to make fewer mistakes than we do. And frankly, that's not hard.

The underlying problem with current human 'software' comes back to the nature of self. Self is, as I've explained (several times, apologies), a story, and stories are of course entirely pliable. Plus we can choose how we interpret them – what I read as comedy, you might experience as tragedy. As a result, a lot of our decisions are based on a mix of those fictions that we've woven about ourselves, what we happen to be feeling at any given moment, and dubious news sourced from that bastion of half-truths and downright lies known as social media. No wonder we're mucking the world up (to put it mildly). So, wouldn't it be better to let someone else make those decisions for us?

This 'hacking of humanity' is already happening in medicine, with many of us hooked up to wearable sensors that monitor our blood sugar, oxygen levels, heart rate, which can then, via an app, advise us on better diet or exercise plans. Or even, in the case of a friend's husband, prevent him going into a diabetic coma. Research shows that Facebook can already outperform our own minds based on our history of 'likes'; occasional but hilarious 'Wish' misses aside, it knows better than we do what we want and happily gives it to us. Kindle already monitors our reading; not just in terms of subject matter (to determine which similar novels to offer us) but the speed at which we read different sections, and when we abandon books altogether. Imagine, suggests Harari, if Kindle could also monitor how each sentence affected blood pressure and heart rate? If it could collect data on what made us angry or sad? All it would take is an upgrade with face recognition and biometric sensors – tech that's already in common use – and Amazon would be able to read you while you read.

Harari imagines – as I painted in the previous section – an omniscient network in which, granted access to all our devices, Google would be able to track our health, our bank balance, even our sex life, and make decisions for us accordingly. And, as he puts it, Google wouldn't be swayed by self-deceptions or misled by 'cooked-up stories', because Google's memory would be fact, not interpretation. So it would be able to tell us what to eat, who to hook up with, even how to vote, because it would represent our dietary requirements, our sexual preferences, our political opinions based on tracked past choices and predicted future need, rather than how we happen to be feeling that day and the few memories we can dredge up, which will in any case be skewed.

For our future self, this will be – hard as it is to accept it – an improvement. We will, thanks to algorithms, be happier and healthier. And not just that, the world will be happier and healthier as well, its future not doomed but assured. Yes, buckle up. Because now, I'm going to suggest, accepting that self isn't singular – that it is playable, multiple, fallible – isn't just about justifying my noodling around on Twitter and using Insta filters to get rid of my smile lines, nor is it about AI producing 'better' election results.

It's about saving humankind.

The hero's last journey

Let me state from the off that I do not fancy Tom Cruise and I never have. Not flipping vodka bottles behind the bar in *Cocktail*, nor as baby-faced Joel Goodman in teen fulfilment vehicle *Risky Business*, not even as Maverick in *Top Gun*, saving America in a dog fight before cruising into the sunset on his silver dream machine. Especially not the last one – I'm military-averse and, anyway, more of a 'Goose' kind of a girl. But as I sat down to the opening credits of the 2022 sequel *Top Gun: Maverick* and what I assumed would be no more than a nostalgia trip, I found myself falling. Not for Tom, but for Maverick and what he represented: a hero who might just save us all in what was then, and still is, undoubtedly, one of the shittiest times for Britain in history. So moved, so invested was I, that I went back again the following day, just to grasp again at that suggestion of hope, that promise that good can triumph over evil, thanks to a singular, gifted man.

I would have gone back a third time had I not reminded myself that one of the things I'm currently researching is how it's this obsession with heroes, with 'chosen one' narratives and maverick protagonists, that means we won't actually be able to save the world at all. Because saving the world requires *all* of us to act, rather than rely on someone 'special', or even on the 'ordinary' kid who manages to perform some extraordinary feat (my preferred oeuvre, given my own mediocrity in most areas). It relies on us shunting ourselves from the centre of our own narratives and seeing ourselves instead as part of a collective. To remind ourselves, like Monty Python or the Derry Girls, that we *are* all individuals, but we're inextricably linked as well; we are small parts in a massive collective.

And the trick to doing this? It comes back, again, to shattering that illusion that self is singular and seizing on it as an opportunity to get connected. If we can do that, and only if we can do that, then we might save not just our declining mental health (I'll explain in a moment), but the human race as well. No biggie then. And how will our utopian future self pull off this brilliant trick? It will work, consciously, to quiet that very section of the brain that insists on telling us that we're both authentic and special, that narrates that 'story of self'.

Quieting the left-brain narrator

Individuality – the belief that we're a single, unique being and remain that same being over time – *has* served us well. It has been a survival tool; it has helped each of us achieve things (why bother doing anything if it's a different self that will get to reap the rewards?), which in turn has led to incredible scientific process. But, in our connected world, it is now profoundly maladaptive. For neuropsychologist

Chris Niebauer, it's at the heart of our mental health crisis, leading to jealousy and shame at the milder end of the spectrum, and anxiety and depression at the far extreme. Ecologist Tom Oliver agrees, likening it to the body's drive to seek out fatty food, resulting in obesity. In his terms, what used to be a survival instinct is now destructive, and not just for each of us as humans, but for our entire race and planet. Because it is this rampant individualism that has led us to climate crisis – all of us, presumably, believing that someone else should be the one to have to make the sacrifice. So we need to conquer what Oliver calls that 'self delusion' if we want to not just thrive, but survive at all. We need to tap back into empathy, into our universal connected-ness, and see ourselves not as a snazzy tapestry, but as a single thread in that tapestry, which outside the fabric has no meaning at all.

So how do we do that?

The answer lies back where we started – in the brain.

Remember when I said that self was a story that we tell ourselves about ourselves? (You'd better – I've said it often enough.) That comes down the left side of the brain, which is our narrator – or, perhaps more accurately what psychologist Michael Gazzaniga, who first worked on split-brain experiments, coined the 'interpreter' – and the side that does that sorting act of 'me' and 'not me'. The right side is more experiential; it feels things and sees things – things that are happening now – but it's only when the left brain gets in on the act that those things begin to take on meaning, and we can weave them into the story. So our future self is going to need to shut the left-hand side up for a bit, or circumvent it, and let the right-hand side – the side that also, incidentally, controls gratitude – do its thing. We will need to do some 'brain training'.

For Chris Niebauer, the first step in the process is being aware of the interpreter and seeing it as just that – one way of reading a situation. As with cognitive behavioural therapy, the trick is to then to decide whether to accept that interpretation or to reject it, to dismiss it as 'just my opinion' rather than 'the way it is'. That feels a little facile, because it's hard to dismiss one's reaction to genuine abuse as 'just an opinion'. But I get his point. On a general level, I've found this to be a useful tool, as has my teenager (Mean Girls are as much a staple of adolescent life as makeovers). But how else can our future selves achieve this, and, more, achieve a better sense of connectedness? How will they engender a sense of being a single thread or a tiny cog in the massive wheel that is not just humankind but Planet Earth? Of being that 'lumpy blue sweater' that Anne Hathaway (yes! Her again!) wore in *The Devil Wears Prada*. And, more than that, how will they put it into practice? Because understanding theoretically that 'the self doesn't exist' or 'this is just my left brain talking' isn't the same as being able to 'feel' it, and then to capitalise on it.

Well, first, there's this marvellous thing called the Overview Effect.

〉 〉 〉 〉 〉 〉

Coined by Frank White in 1987, the 'Overview Effect' is a term for the shift in awareness of astronauts after they've seen the Earth from far away – with its borders dissipated, its conflicts gone. Suddenly they get it; they get that Earth is tiny and fragile, and worth, then, protecting. Now, most of us will never have this experience – to date, fewer than seven hundred humans have made it into space. But there are ways, suggests Jeffrey Kluger in *Time* magazine, to achieve something, if not on the same level, at least in a similar way: by gazing at nature, or at those facets of nature that inspire awe – sunsets, the stars, mountains, the ocean, the Grand Canyon.

Tom Oliver agrees that it's going to be vital that we reconnect with nature, encouraging us to seek outdoor experiences so that we can foster an 'ecological' sense of self. So our future self is going to get its outdoors fix more deeply and more regularly than even the most devoted (and vocal) wild swimmers like me do today. They're going to forest bathe, to adopt allotments, and to nurture patches of greenery wherever they can be encouraged. They're going to, by seeking it out – from the urban fox to coastal otters – fertilise and nurture that sense of connection with nature every day.

This is just the start though. Our 'everybody' will also need to do some serious work on its Westernised brain to get to a more Buddhist concept of 'non-self', beyond simply reminding themselves that 'this is just my opinion'. The methods? The three 'm's (I just made that up; don't Google it): meditation, mindfulness and microdosing.

ᛁ ᛁ ᛘ ᛘ ᛘ ᛘ

I know, I know. I was as sceptical as you probably are at this point that drugs and what I've habitually dismissed as 'woo-woo' are the answer to anything, let alone the future of the self and, by implication, the planet, but hear me out.

Let's start with, arguably, the least controversial: meditation and its younger cousin mindfulness.

For thousands of years, countless people (admittedly I'm not one of them) have understood that meditation can have a profound effect on one's mental health, reducing anxiety and boosting a sense of wellbeing. Now neuroscience has again caught up and confirmed it. The brains of meditators look different to those of non-meditators. Because meditation works by – surprise, surprise! – boosting activity in the right-hand brain – the 'being' bit rather than the 'doing' bit. By meditating we focus on a sense of 'here and now' rather than 'earlier on' or 'tomorrow'; on 'what' rather than 'why'. It also dampens activity in the left of the prefrontal cortex (the bit that deals with self), and in the amygdala (the bit that deals with negative feelings and fear).

Great, you say, ten minutes of Calm app and omming a day and our future self can save the planet? Well, not quite. But if meditation's function is to dampen the 'Me! Me! Me!' left brain and open up the right, it should also loosen up our rigid thinking, potentially shifting and squeezing our preconceived ideas and making us more 'open'. Like mindfulness, which works by fostering a deliberate awareness of the here and now, meditation doesn't require us to

completely block out those narrating thoughts and
negative emotions (which is apparently where I've
been going wrong, imagining I could switch my
consciousness off entirely and then, when I didn't,
declaring myself a meditation failure and trying
roller derby instead). Instead, it recognises them as
just that – mere thoughts – again potentially allowing us to alter our views, and, if enough of us do it,
to be more in tune with each other. This is, I admit, a
bit of a long shot, and even if it hits, a long-term fix,
but I'll take any solution going – including, potentially, drugs.

Okay, so another caveat: I have taken psychedelic
drugs in the past (sorry, Mum). Mushrooms once at
an undergrad party (I laughed a lot, and loved everyone a lot). Acid twice (up Arthur's Seat in Edinburgh
on the last night of the Fringe in 1991, and then a
year or so later with my then best friend in Paris;
both, again, involved a lot of laughing, a lot of
loving everyone, and a lot of noticing how incredibly
green grass was). While it isn't exactly a psychedelic
– the sense of 'altered reality' is far lower – MDMA
has a similar effect, eliciting a rush of both serotonin
(the 'happy' hormone) and oxytocin (the 'love'
hormone associated with empathy and bonding),
causing euphoria and a great sense of togetherness,

as anyone who was part of the nineties rave scene can tell you (though I wouldn't know because the one time I took it I threw up within ten minutes and went home in a sweaty sulk – again: sorry, Mum). So yes, I am more receptive to this idea than many of you might be. But science is behind me here.

Psychopharmacologists have recently revived the once-outlawed acid tests of the sixties to find that drugs like psilocybin (the psychedelic in some mushrooms), acid and MDMA can all have a game-changing effect on the brain. As Michael Pollan investigates in the book and now Netflix miniseries *How to Change Your Mind*, compared to traditional pharmacological treatments, which act on symptoms not cause, large doses of MDMA can switch off the fear and pain associated with traumatic memories of things like abuse, allowing some abuse victims, or others with PTSD, to address those memories and see themselves differently. Psilocybin can do the same for late-stage cancer patients, helping them to make peace with their fate.

Even in 'healthy' people, psychedelics engender a greater sense of experiential 'being' over 'doing' – if you've ever listened to anyone on a trip, you'll know they lose their ability to interpret and thus narrate what's happening other than describing what they see or feel right now. They can also provide profound 'mystical experiences', which can, like MDMA, shift the way we relate to the world and each other, making us more aware of how we're connected. (And if you're rolling your eyes at that, let me assure you what constitutes a 'mystical experience' in these studies is quantified and comes in a handy checklist.) Effectively, all of these suppress that left-hand sense of self, breaking down the stories we've told ourselves in the past and opening us up to new ways of seeing, including that we're all actually connected.

Of these, MDMA, which has been so successful in treating PTSD as well as addiction, is likely to be the first to be legalised. A fact that might worry you, and your future self. After all, large doses of any psychedelic can be, even with scientific backing, slightly scary; 'losing ourselves' isn't an attractive prospect to all of us, however potentially beneficial. The thing is, we don't need to go that far. In order to protect humanity, our future self won't need to lose its 'self' completely; it will just need to, as Oliver puts it, 'tweak' its worldview. In which case, wouldn't it make sense to tweak the dose?

'I feel more mindful all the time.'
'I view things more positively.'

'It doesn't numb me like antidepressants did; it opens me up.'
'It's like when you really "get there" with meditation.'
'You realise that your small self can be met with compassion and that opens you up to the bigger sense of being part of this massive universe.'

These are all testimonies from friends who regularly microdose either LSD or, more commonly, psilocybin. They haven't had those profound psychedelic 'mystical experiences', at least this time (all have – full disclosure – in the past used one or both in more 'macro' doses), but they have all felt more aware of the 'here and now' of things. They have all felt more of a sense of being 'part of this massive universe', which is, while not planet-saving on its own, a big step in the right direction.

Or is it so large a step? We already use plants to alter our brains on a daily basis – tobacco and caffeine. And while tobacco, largely because of the way it's ingested, is hardly an advert for healthy drug use, it shouldn't be such an enormous leap to imagine us swallowing a microscopic sliver of mushroom with our morning coffee. Note, for legal reasons, I'm not saying *you* should go out and do this, just that our future self will do, along with a daily dose of nature and meditation. Because COP 2020 wasn't the fix-all any of us hoped for, and not even Greta Thunberg can save us now. We *all* need to act, and to do so we need to recognise ourselves as threads in the tapestry. And – praise be! – by training its brain in the ways I've detailed, our utopian future self will be able to do just that.

This future self – our 'everybody' – is a triumph. On top of using our playable nature to our own and everyone else's advantage, and while allowing machines to control the parts of life that machines can do better, this future self will use the freed-up time and brainspace to maximise their connections to everyone around them. Meditation and mindfulness will become as quotidian as morning coffee; microdosing will not just be legalised but promoted. Nature will flourish as we cultivate our relationship with it, knowing it does us good. Raves will make a comeback as our clever self recognises how music and dancing further strengthen the threads that connect us. Best of all, by quieting their left brain long enough and often enough, our future self will take every step it can to act in the interests of community, on a local and a global scale.

The world will, through 'play' and 'brain training', be saved.

Stories of self

I admitted at the beginning that I came at this subject as a writer not a psychologist, as if that was
some kind of Achilles heel, or at least a dicky knee.
But it turns out that books, and fiction in particular,
might be yet another way to get us better connected.
Both writing them – this is, surely, the great joy of
a novelist, that we get to play both our 'selves' and
leave those same selves behind as we take on the
guise of others – and reading them.

The wonderful Francis Spufford, in his seminal
The Child That Books Built, puts it like this: 'Be a
Roman soldier, said a book by Rosemary Sutcliffe.
Be an urchin in Georgian London, said a Leon
Garfield [. . .] Be an Egyptian child beside the Nile,
be a rabbit on Watership Down [. . .] Be a King. Be
a slave. Be Biggles.'

And, as well as allowing us to try on new lives for
size – lives we might adopt – fiction can trigger our
sense of empathy and help us, says novelist Mohsin
Hamid, 'investigate the space between the ones and
the zeroes'. It can allow us to be baffled; remind us
not to judge. Fiction can, in other words, help us

acknowledge the non-binary nature of humans. The plasticity of self.

And so, for my future utopian self, I see stories with Gatsbyesque protagonists who are magpies and chameleons but no less relatable for that.

I see stories that address the metaverse and paint a version of our avatar-inhabited future that is not inevitably dystopian.

I see stories that use, as this book does at times, the second person 'you', tacitly acknowledging the dialogic nature of self. Or rather, *more* stories, as what was once a rare narrative technique is now making its way onto bookshelves in the guise of both literary prizewinners and genre fiction. A trend I suspect is related to our fast-changing nature of self.

I see stories that refuse linear inevitability and a discernible end.

I even see stories that, as Virginia Woolf dared to dream, use first person plural: a 'we' that is decidedly more than royal, and yet relates not to a chorus, as in Jeffrey Eugenides' *The Virgin Suicides*, but to a single character. Annie Ernaux's *The Years* has a suggestion of this, though the French original uses the pronoun 'on' as well as 'nous', the former of which could equally be translated as 'one', or that universalising 'you', rather than 'we'. Though both these examples do at least engender a sense of the collective.

Above all, I see stories with a vast cast of narrators (I promised a crowd scene, didn't I?) who work together to find the holy grail, in whatever shape that might take, and save the world. Because, however hard Hollywood, or even writers like me, try to convince us, no singular hero in the Joseph Campbell mould is going to step up and rescue us; it's time for Maverick to finally retire.

Self Reflections

So here are our two versions of the future self:

1. The 'Nobody', who is doomed by their vanity, their fickleness, and their inability to even see what it is that they're doing.
2. The 'Everybody', who recognises and embraces that nebulous nature of self, who works to foster those inherent connections, that 'dialogic' nature, and in doing so redeems not just their self but the world.

So am I going to start microdosing? Probably not. I am, after all, a lightweight. I don't drink (half a glass of Cava renders me insensible and, within half an hour, hungover and full of regret) and I was once literally floored by a niacin tablet. Though I've re-downloaded the Calm app and taken myself off Hinge, so there's a chance I'll be meditating sometime soon.

Because of course, in this great adventure of our future self, I choose the utopian version. I choose hope. I choose to embrace nature, as well as my nature, and the inevitability of our digital future, knowing that this isn't the *Blade Runner* hell it's painted, but a potential paradise. Of course, I would say this. I'm both a natural Pollyanna, and, on Rita Carter's scale of those 'families of selves', hugely multiple. I'm also boringly lower middle-class (or 'technical middle-class' according to the BBC's most recent Class Calculator), and thus desperate to be something – anything – else. And I love social media – you will have to wrest my iPhone out of my cold dead hands before I give it up.

I realise, though, that the idea of this second self – this utopian Everybody – ignores some of the context we are currently living through. It is hard, after all, to feel so irrepressibly positive when so many are struggling to put food on the table, to heat their homes, to stay alive in such a polarised society in the face of relentless abuse. Being one's 'selves' could be seen as a luxury compared to just being at all. But, ever the optimist, I also believe that it's important to try. That a single step is better than no steps at all.

My quest for 'self'

The morning goes like this:

I reach across the vacant space in my double bed, check my iPhone or iPad for Facebook notifications: Who has messaged Me? Who has tagged Me? More importantly, who has 'liked' Me?

I post a status update about Me. I flick to Twitter to over-share my waking thoughts, because everyone needs to hear what *I* have to say. I flick back, change my profile picture to one that better shows off my hard-won weight loss, better reflects the positive Me I am today – a selfie signing books at Hay. Famous Me! Successful Me!

Look at Me!

I pull on a dress that reveals my surgically altered cleavage. I coat my hair in products that tame my grandmother's curls; I paint on concealer that hides my grandfather's dark undereye circles, mascara that promises the look of fake lashes while proclaiming on its packaging 'They're Real', blusher that suggests I may just be in post-coital flush. And all the while I gaze at my reflection in one of the too-many mirrors that adorn my bedroom walls, or the oh-so-con-venient cameras on my iPhone, iPad, MacBook Air.

Do I sound vain? Self-obsessed? Shallow?

Yes.

Do I feel guilty? Ashamed? Adolescent?

No.

Because self is a valid obsession and, while it may be narcissistic, it isn't solipsistic. My self requires an other, not to tell me I matter and to make me feel better, but to exist at all, both in 'real life' and on the page. I know, now, that my 'I' is a 'we', and that this 'we' is part of a gigantic structure – one I and all of us need to find ways to better connect with in the not-at-all distant future if the human race is to have any kind of future at all.

We can't turn back time, nor would we really want to: there's far too much to lose. The trick is to work out how to embrace the gains and mitigate against any losses. So, I exhort you: take pleasure in the metamorphoses of friends and strangers, find ways to connect – in that space between the zeroes and the ones – and above all, stop worrying about 'the real me', because, as I hope I've made clear, it just doesn't exist.

Instead set a path for that utopian future self, and do it boldly and fearlessly, because (you're welcome) I've already slain the dragons that would declare you doomed.

Further Reading
(the utopianish sort)

Al-Kadhi, Amrou, *Life as a Unicorn* (Fourth Estate, 2019)

Baggini, Julian, *The Ego Trick* (Granta, 2012)

Carter, Rita, *Multiplicity* (Little, Brown, 2008)

Gergen, Kenneth, *The Saturated Self* (Basic Books, 1992)

Harari, Yuval Noah, *Homo Deus* (Vintage, 2016)

Hood, Bruce, *The Self Illusion* (Constable, 2012)

Lunbeck, Elizabeth, *The Americanization of Narcissism* (Harvard University Press, 2014)

Niebauer, Chris, *No Self, No Problem* (Hierophant Publishing, 2019)

Oliver, Tom, *The Self Delusion* (Weidenfeld & Nicolson, 2020)

Pollan, Michael, *How to Change Your Mind* (Penguin Books, 2018)

Spufford, Francis, *The Child That Books Built* (Faber & Faber, 2018)

About the Series

Each volume in the FUTURES Series presents a vision imagined by an accomplished writer and subject expert. The series seeks to publish a diverse range of voices, covering as wide-ranging a view as possible of our potential prospects. Inspired by the brilliant 'To-Day and To-Morrow' books from a century ago, we ask our authors to write in a spirit of pragmatic hope, and with a commitment to map out potential future landscapes, highlighting both beauties and dangers. We hope the books in the FUTURES Series will inspire readers to imagine what might lie ahead, to figure out how they might like the future to look, and, indeed, to think about how we might get there.

Professor Max Saunders and Dr Lisa Gee, series originators, University of Birmingham

The FUTURES Series was originally conceived by Professor Max Saunders and Dr Lisa Gee, both of whom work at the University of Birmingham. Saunders is Interdisciplinary Professor of Modern Literature and Culture and the author of *Imagined Futures: Writing, Science, and Modernity in the To-Day and To-Morrow book series*, 1923–31 (OUP 2019), and Gee is Assistant Professor in Creative Writing and Digital Media and Research Fellow in Future Thinking. To find out more about their Future Thinking work visit www.birmingham.ac.uk/futures

Author's Acknowledgements

There are, as I said at the beginning, myriad brilliant minds to whom I owe a debt for their innovative thinking on self that has shaped this book, as well as several novels and my doctorate. Their ideas, and names, litter this text. In addition, I would like to thank Dr Lisa Gee, Professor Emerita Julia Green, Professor Tracy Brain and Steve Voake, who have all played a part in shaping this, and shaping me.